The World of Nature

WILDFLOWERS

GALLERY BOOKS
An Imprint of W. H. Smith Publishers Inc.
112 Madison Avenue
New York City 10016

This edition first published in U.S.
in 1990 by Gallery Books,
an imprint of W.H. Smith Publishers, Inc.
112 Madison Avenue, New York, New York 10016

ISBN 0-8317-9580-8

Printed and bound in Spain

For rights information about the photographs in
this book please contact:

The Image Bank
111 Fifth Avenue, New York, N.Y. 10003

Producer: Solomon M. Skolnick
Author: Ann Reilly
Design Concept: Leslie Ehlers
Designer: Ann-Louise Lipman
Editor: Terri L. Hardin
Production: Valerie Zars
Photo Researcher: Edward Douglas
Assistant Photo Researcher: Robert Hale

**Preceding page:
Native to Thailand, *Paphiopedilum callosum* is one of the most beautiful wildflowers. Called the lady-slipper orchid because many consider the lip to be shaped like a maiden's shoe, its long-lasting blooms start to appear in late winter. Opposite: From late winter to late spring, California poppies (*Eschscholtzia californica*) adorn the hillsides along the California coast. The golden yellow petals are as delicate as tissue paper.**

Wildflowers, the hardy plants that thrive along roadsides, in swamps and deserts, and on mountaintops, are sometimes called "native" plants. This term is not really correct: while all wildflowers were indeed native plants at sometime or another, their present distribution has been greatly influenced by human wandering. What is native to Asia might today be a wildflower in Europe; what is native to North America could be a wildflower in Australia, or vice versa. Some wildflowers have received intervention from man and have been transformed into formal garden plants. Others remain truly wild, growing only with the help of nature.

Their world is vast and fascinating: From the first skunk cabbages of spring, through the daisies of summer, to the last goldenrod of fall, wildflowers come in every imaginable size, shape and color, and their parentage derives from numerous and different plant families.

Top to bottom: Native Americans ate the foliage of the California poppy (*Eschscholtzia californica*) and used its root as a painkiller. A meadow of California poppies is fragrant. The poppies were named after Johann Eschscholtz, who visited California in 1815 from Russia. A Texas prairie comes to life in spring when Texas bluebonnets and golden coreopsis burst into color. Coreopsis is often called tickseed because the seeds are flat, narrow, and have two winglike projections extending from their sides.

Lupinus latifolius subalpinus, a native of the Alaska mountains, and *Lilium columbianum*, Columbia lily, whose home reaches into northern California, meet in a Pacific northwest wildflower garden. Below: The hills are often alive with the sight of wildflowers, such as those found growing on this Swiss mountainside.

Black-eyed Susan (*Rudbeckia fulgida*) is native to the midwest U.S., but was accidentally introduced to the eastern U.S. in a bag of clover seed. It spread quickly to cover fields and roadsides, filling the summer with its bright golden flowers. Below: Annual sunflower, or *Helianthus annuus*, may be the state flower of Kansas and native to the U.S. and Mexico, but it was also known to the Incas, who revered it as a sun god. Opposite: Cardinal flower (*Lobelia cardinalis*) is a favorite plant of hummingbirds. Insects cannot reach inside its long, tubular flowers, leaving the job of fertilization to the pollen that rubs off on the hummingbirds' heads.

Above, left to right: Sometimes called blue-eyed Mary, *Collinsia heterophylla* was named for Philadelphia botanist Zaccheus Collins in the late 1700's. Although called wild hyacinths, there are a number of plants, such as wood hyacinth (botanically *Endymion hispanicus*), that are not hyacinths at all. Native from southern Alaska to the eastern U.S. and as far south as Mexico, shooting star (*Dodecatheon pulchellum*) blooms in late spring or early summer, depending on the weather. Below: Wherever large, graceful colonies of bluets (*Houstonia lanciolata*) are found, bees and butterflies won't be far behind.

No matter how adverse the climate may seem, there is a flowering plant that will grow, adding color, charm and sometimes curiosity to its surroundings. There is no more enchanting a scene or no more brilliant a view, whether you're walking through the woods, driving on a parkway, or hiking on a hillside, than to come across a mass of wildflowers. But wildflowers offer more than fields of color and fragile-looking-but-sturdy plants that poke their way up through the forest floor. Many have a delicious fragrance that you can enjoy as you walk among them. Find plantings of Canada mayflower, clover, milkweed, violets, water lilies and day lilies if you want to savor their fragrance, or stroll past evening primrose and dame's rocket at night.

Some wildflowers, though, have an unpleasant fragrance. No one needs to explain how the skunk cabbage got its name!

Over a million miles of Texas roadsides have been planted with wildflowers, primarily the state flower, Texas bluebonnet (*Lupinus subcarnosus*). The spectacle is due in large part to the efforts of Lady Bird Johnson. Below: Legend has it that Norse invaders, attempting to seize a Scottish castle, walked barefoot through a moat that had been drained and filled with thistle. Their cries of pain alerted the Scots. Pictured here is the common, or bull, thistle, *Cirsium lanceolatum*.

Snowy thistle (*Cirsium pastoris*), a native to northern California, southern Oregon and western Nevada, will grow for a year without flowering, bloom the second year, and then die after dropping seeds to continue the cycle. Below: There are a number of wild morning glories, or bind-weeds, in the *Convolvulus* genus. All have lovely flowers that open at sunrise and close by early afternoon. Opposite: At least 35 species of wild roses are native to the U.S., and fossils have been found in Colorado that place them there as long as 40 million years ago.

Enjoying wildflowers can involve more than soaking up their visual beauty and inhaling their fragrance. A study of their names is a history of early naturalists, gardeners and other lovers of wildflowers. *Rudbeckia*, the black-eyed Susan of the roadside, was named for Olaf Rudbeck. This Swedish botanist was teacher to Linnaeus, the man responsible for devising the first scientific approach to naming plants and animals, called binomial nomenclature, in the eighteenth century. Linnaeus went on to name plants for other people, among them *Houstonia*, or bluet, which was named for William Houston, a Scottish surgeon and botanist. (Houston didn't discover the bluet, but Linnaeus liked him and named it for him anyway.)

The Flemish botanist Matthias de l'Obel worked as a physician for King James I in the early seventeenth century, and because of that anglicized his name to Lobel, which in turn led to *Lobelia*, the genus that includes the cardinal flower and great blue lobelia.

Top to bottom: Flax has been known since ancient times as the source of linen. Pictured is wild blue flax, *Linum perenne.* Purslane, or *Portulaca oleracea*, is a common creeper, with flowers that only open in full sun. Grass widow (*Sisyrinchium douglasii*) is a member of the iris family that blooms in spring in dry meadows. The plant name in Greek means "pig grubbing," because wild pigs grub (dig into) the roots.

Above: The common blue violet (*Viola sororia*) is edible; it can be candied or floated on drinks. Right: Evening primroses' flowers open in the evening and remain open until late the next day. They share the genus *Oenothera* with sundrops, which act in the opposite manner, opening in the morning and closing in the afternoon.

An annual, Indian blanket (*Gaillardia ulchella*) is the same color as the blankets woven by the Indians in the Southwest, where it is native. Its coloration has given it a second common name, fire wheel. Below: Gaily colored is a field of golden pea (*Thermopsis montana*) and Indian paint brush (*Castilleja*). Legend says that a Great Spirit gave an American Indian some brushes to paint a sunset that afterward grew into plants.

Fields and roadsides are gracefully covered all summer with the delicate flowers and fernlike foliage of Queen Anne's lace. The flowers can be cut and dried to use for winter decoration. Below: Oswego tea is made from bee balm (*Monarda didyma*), which is sometimes called bergamot.

Preceding page: A ground-hugging relative of the dogwood tree, bunchberry (*Cornus canadensis*) fills in the woodland floor. This page: Although most phlox thrive in the full sun, wild blue phlox (*Phlox divaricata*) grows wild in all 50 states, Canada and Mexico wherever there are moist woods. Below: Scorpionweed is the common name of several plants in the *Phacelia* genus; its flowering stems are coiled like a scorpion's tail when the flowers first open. Opposite: *Trillium grandiflorum*, the largest-flowering trillium, is sometimes called wake robin because it blooms in early spring.

Above, left to right: Dutchmen's breeches (*Dicentra cucullaria*) is also called staggerweed because it is poisonous to cattle. Unique among flowering plants, Indian pipe (*Monotropa uniflora*) has no chlorophyll and relies on fungi that grow on rotting wood and leaves on the forest floor for its survival. *Erythronium albidum* is known by two common names, dog-tooth violet and trout lily, but is related to the lily rather than violet. Below: One of the tiniest irises is *Iris cristata*, or crested iris, which grows in woods and along streams, and blooms in early spring.

Rosebay rhododendron, or great laurel (*Rhododendron maximum*), is one of the largest of evergreen shrubs, reaching heights of 20 feet in wooded areas. For self-protection, its leaves curl under in the winter whenever the temperature drops below freezing. California bluebells (*Campanula prenanthoides*) are unique among bluebells because the style extends so far out beyond the flower.

An American native, *Geranium maculatum* grows in either woods or meadows. It is sometimes called cranesbill because the seed pods resemble the beak of that bird. They split open explosively and cast their seeds for long distances. Below: Flowers take several forms in the genus *Calochortus*. One type, containing the species *albus* (pictured here), is called globe lily or fairy wand for the nodding, rounded flowers.

Above: Fire pinks (*Silene virginica*) are also called catchflies because flies often get stuck in the "spittle" that forms on the leaves and stems. The stickiness of catchflies protects them from crawling insects.
Right: Clumps of butterfly orchids grow amidst the fine foliage of resurrection fern in a shaded wildflower garden. Butterfly orchids are epiphytes, which means that while in the wild they grow on other plants—often high in tree branches—they do not steal nourishment.

The reign of James I was followed by that of Charles I, whose gardeners were the father-and-son team of John and John Tradescant, for whom *Tradescantia*, or spiderwort, is named. The Tradescants were among the first in England to grow the wildflowers discovered in the New World.

When Anne became Queen of England, she challenged her ladies-in-waiting to make a lace as beautiful as one of the plants that grew in her garden. The resulting name was Queen Anne's lace, or wild carrot, which almost 300 years later is still filling fields with its graceful, swaying flower heads.

Pickerelweed, the lovely plant that fills shallow ponds with spikes of blue flowers, dragonflies and bees, was named for Guilo Pontedera, an eighteenth-century botanist who lent his name to the plant's Latin calling, *Pontederia*.

This page: Pitcher plants, which are in the genus *Sarracenia*, thrive in bogs, swamps and low, moist woodlands. Because there is little nourishment in this type of soil, pitcher plants trap insects, perhaps by the stagnant water their leaves hold, and convert their protein into useable nitrogen. Opposite: Foxgloves were first identified as such in 1542; they are in the genus *Digitalis*, for which the heart medication is named.

Although no one is really sure, it is believed that Joe-pye weed was named for an American Indian, Joe Pye, a man who taught the colonists how to use the plant to relieve typhus fever. Two other Americans, Lewis and Clark, who were as interested in discovering new plants as they were new lands, were honored when the wildflowers *Lewisia* and *Clarkia* were named for them.

Because wildflowers have been known since before recorded history, there is a store of lore and legends surrounding them. Greek legends in particular abound with flower origins.

The aster, whose name comes from the Greek word for star, is said to have grown from a god's scattering stardust on the earth. Asters were used on altars to keep evil spirits away.

Native to the southeastern U.S., southern red lilies (*Lilium catesbaei*) grow in bogs and wet pinelands and are therefore sometimes called pine lilies. Below: Native to bogs where there is little nutrition, the Venus fly trap (*Dionae muscipula*) traps insects inside its hinged leaves. Small hairs on the leaf margin trigger the leaf to close when disturbed. About a week later, the plant is ready to catch another fly.

Pliny writes of the anemone (from the Greek word meaning "wind") opening at the beckoning of the wind; another legend says it sprang from the tears shed by Venus when Adonis was slain (although this legend is also associated with the rose). Yarrow, or *Achillea,* was named for Achilles, who was supposed to have brought the plant with him to battle to help cure his soldiers' wounds.

Religion has had its influence on wildflower names, too. Pasque flower was named because it blooms during the Pasch season of Passover and Easter, and Michaelmas daisy because it blooms in late September at the same time as the feast day of St. Michael the Archangel. The three-leaf clover has long been associated with the Trinity and the columbine with the Holy Spirit.

Top to bottom: As a self-defense mechanism against heat, the foliage of bleeding heart (*Dicentra spectabilis*) dies, disappearing by midsummer. Bees and many other insects are attracted to snow plant (*Sarcodes sanguinea*) because of its odor. Snow plant has no chlorophyll; it lives on fungi found in decaying matter on the forest floor. The fine, narrow leaflets of sensitive brier (*Schrankia nuttalis*) close up at the slightest jarring. Plants are thorny and are also called cat's claw. Overleaf: Logan Pass in Glacier National Park, Montana, is alive in spring with the golden hues of (*Erythronium grandiflorum*), the glacier or avalanche lily.

Flame azalea (*Rhododendron calendulaceum*) is a member of the *Rhododendron* genus; this species is deciduous. Below: Known as West Coast rhododendron and California rosebay, *Rhododendron macrophyllum* is native to the Pacific Northwest. Opposite: The eastern slopes of the Cascade Mountains blaze in spring with phlox, Indian paint brush, lupines and mule's ears.

Flower legends live in the games of childhood, passed on from generation to generation. A child may have a buttercup held under his chin to confirm that he likes butter, or pick the petals off a daisy and ask, "She loves me, she loves me not?" And many have looked through a field to find that elusive four-leaf clover in the hopes of receiving good luck.

The beneficial properties of wildflowers have been enshrouded in folklore and superstition. It has been said – although it's probably not true – that hawks used to feed on hawkweed to improve their eyesight, and that sightwort, or celandine, was used by mother swallows to sharpen the eyesight of their young, cure eye infections and enable them to better catch insects. (Until about 300 years ago, men believed such legends and used these wildflowers themselves for improved

Top to bottom: One of several plants commonly known as gentian, *Gentianella cerastioides* blooms high in all mountains of the world but Africa's. Calypso orchid (*Calypso bulbosa*), also called fairy slipper, is found in bogs and cool, mature forests. Canada violet (*Viola canadensis*) grows a foot high, and can be found in forests and along stream banks. Opposite: Wild columbine (*Aquilegia canadensis*) has five petals that stretch back to form spurs where nectar collects.

Opposite: *Diapensia lapponica* can be seen only at high altitudes; it grows in an area around the North Pole as far south as New England, the Alps and Mongolia. Above: The flowers of purple mountain saxifrage (*Saxifraga oppositifolia*) stay open until each of the many stamens mature, one at a time. Alpine forget-me-not (*Eritrichium*) grows wild in the mountains of Alaska, as well as the Rockies, the Himalayas and the Alps.

eyesight.) Bouquets of violets were often given to loved ones, as it was believed that they had amorous powers, and the Scottish have a superstition that if you encircle butter-and-eggs three times, it will break any spell that might have been cast upon you.

The iris, the basis for the *fleur-de-lis,* the French sign of royalty, has also symbolized heraldry. (It is sometimes even called "flag" because of the way it flutters in the wind.) The flower is named after the Greek word for rainbow because it is available in so many colors. In Japan, the iris is a symbol of masculinity, just as peach blossoms represent femininity.

Preceding page: Where the sun beats down and the soil is dry, and little else will thrive, sunflowers (*Helianthus annuus*) have no problem surviving. Above: Golden rainbow cactus (*Echinocereus pectinatus neomaxicanus*), like many cacti, has ribs that expand and contract depending on the amount of water the plant is storing. The spines shade the stem and help to prevent water loss. Below: A desert plant, *Fouguieria splendens* looks dead most of the time. Opposite: The flowers of saguaro (*Carnegia giganteus*) open at night and close the following afternoon. These post-like cacti can reach heights of 60 feet.

The Quakers gave names to two wildflowers: Quaker rouge, or mullein, because young Quaker girls, who were not allowed to wear makeup, rubbed the leaves on their cheeks to make them red; and bluets, or Quaker Ladies, who used to wear white hats reminiscent of the small flowers.

The history of man, especially in the ages of the great explorations, can be told by studying the origins of wildflowers. One of the great European explorers, Marco Polo, is said to have brought the day lily to Europe from Asia. From there it traveled across the Atlantic and spread over North America. Today there is hardly a place in the world where you won't find day lilies growing.

When the early European settlers came to America, they brought with them some of their favorite plants, such as buttercups, chicory, clover, ox-eye daisy, loosestrife, Queen Anne's lace, tansy, violet and yarrow, to grow in their doorstep gardens for medicinal use, as well as to ease some of their homesickness.

Top to bottom: The tubular flowers of Indian paint brush (*Castilleja chromosa*) are pollinated by what brushes off on the heads of hummingbirds and swarming insects. Mexican poppy (*Eschscholtzia mexicana*) is a close relative of the California poppy, but is a little smaller and the flowers are a little darker. The spring desert is colored with Mexican poppy, owl's clover (*Orthocarpus purpurascens*) and apricot mallow (*Sphaeralcea coulteri*). Opposite: Each leaf of desert gold (*Linanthus aurens*) is so deeply divided that the leaf looks like a tuft of grass.

Above, left to right: The *Calochortus* genus contains species with different types of flowers. The *Kennedyi* (desert mariposa), pictured here, are brightly colored and sometimes marked in contrasting colors. When it is dry, purple mat is hard to see (*Nama demissum*), but when there is rain, plants will be covered with a profusion of flowers. *Calochortus flexuosus*, pictured here, has cup-shaped flowers and is called star tulip. Below: A desert annual blooming in spring, desert five spot (*Eremalche rotundifolia*) is found in California, Arizona and New Mexico.

The Spanish brought plants to the south and west; the French to Canada; the English and Dutch to the northeast. As settlers moved west, so did the new plants, some brought intentionally and others accidentally transported in clothing, on wagon wheels or behind the ears of the family dog.

By the same token, as the New World was explored, many wildflowers, reported to have medicinal qualities, filled ships headed for the European market. Many plants unknown to Europe came to its shores to remain and are still prized in its gardens. In fact, one might view the flowers in the English countryside, and find cardinal flower, lewisia, mariposa lilies and phlox – all originally wildflowers from the United States! The British have even made a cherished flower out of goldenrod, even though most Americans still think of it as an irritating weed.

Above: When it rains, the flowers of *Langloisia punctata* are so large, they seem out of proportion to the rest of the plant; in dry spells, however, the plants themselves almost disappear. The common names are spotted langloisia or lilac sunbonnet. Right: The flowers of the claret cup cactus (*Echinocereus triglochidiatus*) close at night. The spines are actually modified leaves and collect water from the dew.

Once Australia was explored, there were even more plants for wildflower gardens, including sunray, sand flower, globe amaranth and strawflower. The South Africans have given us many beautiful flowers as well, including treasure flower, ice plant, gerbera and African daisy.

Probably the largest family of flowers – one that includes wild and domesticated flowers alike – is that of Orchidaceae, or orchid family. While such tropical exotics as the now-cultivated genera *Cattleya* and the *Vanilla* (from which we derive vanilla beans) most often come to mind, representatives of this robust family can be found the world over. *Calypso bulbosa*, or fairy slipper, flowers from May to July in northern regions of the U.S. as well as Canada, and the bee orchid (*Ophrys apifera*) of southern Europe lures male bees to propagate it by mimicking the look and scent of the female. The orchid flower is distinguished by three sepals that often resemble petals; three

This page: Prickly pear cactus (*Opuntia macrocentra*) blooms in late spring and early summer in deserts and dry grasslands. The flat, oval pads of prickly pear cactus are actually its stems, which sprawl to form dense mats. It is eaten by peccaries, deer and cattle.

petals, of which the middle petal is a modified lip that may carry a spur or sac. The orchid gives its viewer great pleasure whenever it is encountered.

Although the orchid family has more species, it is the Rosaceae, or rose family, that shows the greatest diversity. One tends, for the most part, to think of rose family members simply as the fragrant, sometimes small blossoms that are found growing in all climates. Actually, the family includes trees, such as hawthorns; and fruit, such as apples, peaches, and strawberries. Distinguishing rose family members are their flowers – usually five-petalled around many stamens – and rich foliage with serrated edges.

Other families of familiar wildflowers are Asteraceae (the sunflower family, which also includes goldenrod), Scrophu- lariaceae (the snapdragon family, to which butter-and-eggs belongs), Nymphaeceae (the water lily family) and Liliaceae (the lily family, which also includes false hellebore). These are but a few; there are many, many more!

Top to bottom: Known as dagger cactus or galloping cactus, *Lemaireocereus gum-mosus* has edible, red, round fruit. Resins from plants known commonly as laudanum or rock rose (*Cistus ladanifer*) are used in the perfume industry. Like most plants whose deep taproots can reach far down into the soil for water, white prickly poppy (*Argemone hispida*) is very drought-resistant.

Wildflowers have a story all their own to tell about the marvels and tenacity of the plant kingdom and the symbiotic relationship that exists between plants and other creatures.

Wildflowers provide nectar for hummingbirds, bees and other insects. As the birds and insects feed, they carry pollen from one plant to another.

Some wildflowers attract insects because of the shape, the color, or the aroma of the flower, be it pleasant or not. Purple trillium, for example, has a foul aroma that attracts the carrion fly that pollinates it.

Few wildflowers pollinate without the help of insects. Without pollination there are few seeds produced; without seeds, no new wildflowers. When the Australians first brought red clover to their shores to feed their cattle, they had no success with the plant, for they forgot to import bumblebees! And you'll never find a monarch butterfly where you can't find milkweed growing.

The daisylike blooms of treasure flower (*Gazania rigens*) appear all summer but close at night and on cloudy days. Below: Natives of South Africa, members of the *Ursinia* genus are annual wildflowers that have scented foliage.

Lampranthus criniflorus, a native of South Africa, is one of a group of plants known as ice plants. Below: At one time, all ice plants were included in the genus *Mesembryanthemum*; today, botanists have divided them into at least nine different genera. Overleaf: Ice plant (*Mesembryanthemum crystallinum* is pictured here) got its name from the small lumps on its leaves that glisten in the sunlight like ice. Ice plants now grow wild all over California, the Canary Islands and the Mediterranean.

The flowers of some asters, buttercups, chicory, fleabane, dandelion, English daisy and others close at night to protect the reproductive parts of the flowers when insects are not flying about and pollinating them. Conversely, night-flowering catch fly, bladder campion and evening primrose open at night when the night-flying moths that feed on them are active.

Most perennials, and all annuals, increase by seeds. Seeds can be carried by the wind for many miles or only a few feet, depending on their size and shape. Birds carry seeds away from their favorite plants, dropping some as they fly off. Sticky seeds and seeds with burrs have been transported far by such range animals as buffalo, antelope and deer. Seeds can float on

Top to bottom: *Fragaria chiloensis*, beach or wild strawberry, is one of the parents of the garden strawberry. Not a primrose at all, beach evening primrose (more correctly called beach sundrops) is a day-blooming, low-growing plant native to the Oregon coast; its botanical name is *Oenothera cheiranthifolia*. This wild rose (*Rosa rugosa*) is among the toughest, growing in pure sand and not minding strong ocean breezes. In fall, attractive red fruits called "hips" appear.

Lilium michauxii has a number of common names, including wild cap lily and Carolina lily. Most appropriately, it is called Turk's cap lily. This fragrant lily attracts monarch butterflies. Below: *Caltha palustris*, known as marsh marigold, is actually more closely related to the buttercup. Also known as cowslip, it blooms in early spring in marshes and alongside lakes and streams.

water and, by this means, start new colonies of wildflowers further downstream. Ants carry trillium seeds to their nests because they use the coating on the seeds to build their nests. They discard the seeds, which begin to grow wherever they are left.

The setting of seed takes a lot of energy out of plants. When Jack-in-the-pulpit has a lot of available food, it produces two leaves and female flowers to enable it to set seed. When nutrition is low, it produces only male flowers – or no flowers at all – in order to merely survive.

Some seeds can live for decades. Cactus seeds will lie dormant in the desert sand until enough rain falls for them to germinate and grow. Other plants produce tremendous numbers of seeds, almost as if they know that many will be eaten and that not all those that do germinate will survive.

Above, left to right: The blooming catkins of pussy willows (*Slix discolor*) delight children and adults alike. Pussy willows flourish throughout North America. The lady-slipper orchid (*Cypripedium reginae*) is the symbol of the province of Prince Edward Island and state flower of Minnesota. There's no nectar, but the fragrant scent inside the pouch of a yellow lady-slipper orchid attracts insects who—burrowing inside—deposit pollen. Below: Blue waterlily, or *Nymphaea elegans*, is a day-blooming waterlily.

Not all plants need to set seed in order to increase. Some, like silverweed (*Potentilla anserina*) send out long stems – called runners – that start to grow young plants once their ends touch soil. Also, the branches and stems of many plants, when severed from their parent plant, will root and grow.

Some wildflowers are perennials, and although their tops die to the ground over the winter, the roots remain alive and spread underground to increase the size of the colony. These roots vary according to plant. Some plants, such as those of the lily family, grow rhizomes, corms or bulbs. These thick and fleshy roots multiply – sometimes wildly, which accounts for the day lily's worldwide success.

Above: *Nymphaea odirata*, or fragrant waterlily, is native from Canada to Florida and west to the Mississippi. Its floating flowers fill ponds and lakes with a delightful aroma. After the flowers fade, seeds form, float for a while, and sprout when they become waterlogged and fall to the lake floor. Right: The waterlily genus, *Nymphaea*, was named for the mythological nymphs of ancient Greece who lived in ponds and secluded lakes.

Wildflowers have the ingenious ability to adapt to their surroundings. Asters that grow in the shade have large leaves to soak up as much of the available light as possible, while those that grow where it is hot and dry have smaller leaves to keep from drying out too quickly. For a similar reason, chicory leaves are large and unlobed to gather more sunlight where their growing conditions are good, and lobed to save moisture where the soil is poor and dry. The leaves of many wildflowers wilt in the heat so less moisture will be lost through their leaf surfaces, but Joe-pye weed's young leaves are often purple to protect them from sunburn.

Many wildflowers have hairy stems or leaves which help them conserve moisture and better withstand hot and dry days. The spines of cactus, in addition to keeping many animals away from the plants, actually gather dew and shade the stem to conserve water.

Opposite, top to bottom: Widow's tears (*Commelina erecta*) have flowers that last only one day. When the flowerbuds of skunk cabbage (*Lysichiton americanum*) form in late winter, they generate so much heat that they melt the snow around them! This page: One of the best plants to grow by the waterside is yellow flag, or Iris pseudoacorus. A European native, it has become naturalized all over North America. Alaskans chose the forget-me-not (*Myosotis scorpioides*) as their state flower because its reliability and strength reminded them that their early settlers had the same virtues. Overleaf: *Passiflora coccinea*, or scarlet passionflower, is a vine native from Venezuela to Bolivia.

Above left to right: Although *Coelogyne pandurata*, a native of Malaya and Borneo, is called the black orchid, it is a yellow or green orchid with brown or black warty markings. *Miltonias*, or pansy orchids, are native to Central and South America. *Cychnoches ventricosum warscewiczii*, called the swan orchid, is a native of Panama and Costa Rica. Below: Native to Costa Rica and Ecuador, *Trichocentrum tigrinum* is spotted in red like a tiger and has a very prominent lip.

This page: The first Europeans to see and name plants were often the priest-scholars that accompanied the early explorers. For this reason, there is often found religious symbolism in plant names. Passionflower, for example, represents the passion of Christ: The three stigmas of the flower are the nails used to hold Christ to the cross; the five stamens are the wounds with which Christ was inflicted; the fringe is the crown of thorns; the 10 petal-like parts are the apostles, excluding Peter and Judas.

If you want to attract birds to the garden, one of the best ways to do it is with wildflowers. Goldfinches use thistle to make their nests, and hummingbirds are lured by the red flowers of cardinal flower and American columbine.

Many wildflowers, in addition to providing food for birds and insects, provide food for man as well. The leaves of chicory, dandelions, day lilies, violets and wintercress can be used as salad greens; chicory and dandelion roots can also be roasted and used as coffee. Dandelion (from the Old French *dent de lion*, meaning lion's tooth) flowers are also used in wine, as are red clover blooms. Today's carrot developed from Queen Anne's lace, and the roots of day lilies, evening primrose and cattails are also edible and nutritious.

Strelitzia reginae, or bird of paradise, is native to South Africa. Left: From southeast Asia, *Nepenthes albomarginata* is a tropical pitcher plant. The stem, or "pitcher," holds water, has a lid, and traps insects inside.

Outside of the kitchen, tansy has been used for centuries to repel insects; yarrow and geranium roots used as a styptic; orris root used as a fixative in potpourri; and butterfly weed, butter-and-eggs, and mullein are all natural dyes.

When the last flowers of fall have faded and the wildflowers have gone to rest for the winter, they can still be remembered. Cut cattails, as well as the dried flowers or seed pods of other wildflowers such as black-eyed Susan, asters, campion, yarrow, Queen Anne's lace, immortelle, cardoon and thistle, and enjoy them until the wildflower garden comes back into bloom the following spring.

Top to bottom: Known by several different names, *Pyrostegia venusta* may be called flame vine, flame flower, flaming trumpet or golden shower. From Brazil and Paraguay, it can also be seen in southern Florida. Known as nun's orchid or nun's hood orchid, *Phaius tankervilliaw* has clusters of up to 20 flowers that reach four feet in length. It is native to the Himalayas. Lipstick plant is either of two species, *Aeschynanthus pulcher* or *A. radicans*, named for the shape and color of its flower, which looks like a tube of lipstick.

A small tree frog rests in a plant of *Neoregelia*, a bromeliad native to Brazil that now grows throughout tropical America. When the plant is about to flower, the leaves in the center of the plant turn bright red. Below: *Solandra maxima*, also known as chalice vine, cup of gold, gold cup or trumpet plant. It flowers in winter and is native to Mexico.

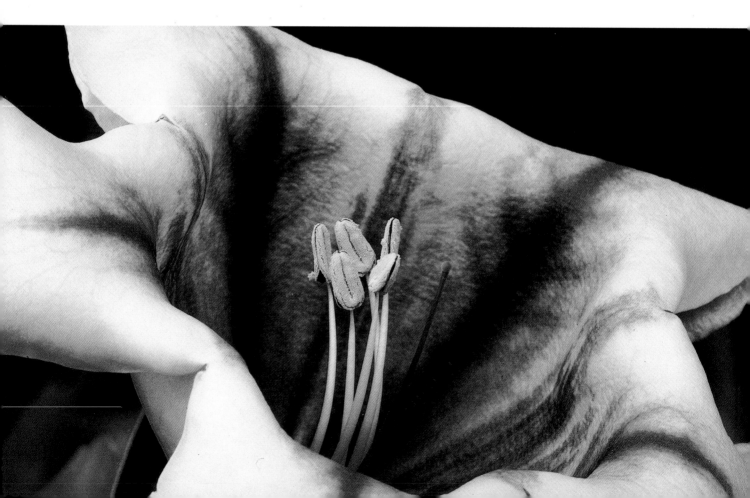

Hibiscus is native to almost every part of the world; all have showy flowers with a prominent central appendage. Some plants are used to make rope, foodstuffs, or medicine. Below: The leaves of *Cochliostema jacobianum* resemble those of a bromeliad. Native to wet lowlands and forests from Costa Rica to Bolivia, the flower clusters reach 12 inches in length.

INDEX OF PHOTOGRAPHY